CHRI...

AN...

C.S. Lewis is renowned as an author of many books on Christianity, as well as for a science fiction trilogy, *The Chronicles of Narnia* and many works of literary criticism.

He was born in Ireland in 1898, gained a Triple First at Oxford and was Fellow and Tutor at Magdalene College 1925–54, when he became Professor of Medieval and Renaissance Literature at Cambridge. He died in November 1963, at his home in Oxford.

Walter Hooper was born in Reidsville, North Carolina, in 1931. He read theology and then lectured on Medieval and Renaissance English at the University of Kentucky.

In 1963 he became companion-secretary to C.S. Lewis, a post he filled for the remaining months of the Professor's life. Still resident in Oxford, Father Hooper is one of the trustees of the C.S. Lewis Estate and a recognized authority on the Professor's works.

C. S. LEWIS

CHRISTIAN REUNION

AND OTHER ESSAYS

EDITED BY WALTER HOOPER

COLLINS
FOUNT PAPERBACKS

William Collins Sons & Co. Ltd
London • Glasgow • Sydney • Auckland
Toronto • Johannesburg

First published in Great Britain in 1990 by Fount Paperbacks
Fount Paperbacks is an imprint of
Collins Religious Division,
part of the Collins Publishing Group
8 Grafton Street, London W1X 3LA

Typeset by Burns & Smith Ltd., Derby.

Printed and bound in Great Britain by
William Collins Sons & Co. Ltd, Glasgow

CONTENTS

INTRODUCTION

In the Preface to *Mere Christianity* C.S. Lewis said: "Ever since I became a Christian I have thought that the best, perhaps the only, service I could do for my unbelieving neighbours was to explain and defend the belief that has been common to nearly all Christians at all times.... The questions which divide Christians from one another often involve points of high theology or even of ecclesiastical history which ought never to be treated except by real experts. I should have been out of my depth in such waters: more in need of help myself than able to help others."

As far as I am able to discover, the essay on "Christian Reunion" is the only sustained piece of writing we have from Lewis on "the questions which divide" the Anglican and the Roman Catholic Churches, and in some instances the other churches as well. I have no idea who prompted him to write it, except that the invitation obviously came from Roman Catholics. I think the appeal must have been very strong, for this division is one of the few subjects Lewis almost never chose to write or talk about. Thus far I have found no one who remembers it, and I can't help but suppose that the essay is being published here for the first time. Even the manuscript of "Christian Reunion" has its own fascination, for it is written on the back of a few surviving leaves of the "Mere Christianity" broadcasts given over the BBC in 1944. I expect this essay was written about the same time.

But "Christian Reunion" is more than a museum piece. When it was discovered after Lewis's death in 1963, it was set aside by his Estate for several reasons. During the 1960s many of the Christian certainties were under attack, and it was feared that anything suggestive of further controversy might divert readers' minds from Lewis's magnificent writings. More than anything, the Second Vatican Council (1962–65) was under way, and it seemed best to wait and see what effect it might have on the relations between the churches.

Not only has Lewis's essay lost none of its relevance, but I think it has more now than when it was written. The "heavenly unity" he wrote about is being sought by nearly *all* the churches, the Non-Conformist and the Orthodox as well as the Roman Catholic and

Anglican. I think the starting point may have been the Vatican Council's powerful "Decree on Ecumenism". It opens with the statement that such divisions as we have "scandalize the world, and damage that most holy cause, the preaching of the Gospel to every creature", and it goes on to say that the Lord of Ages nevertheless pours out both the grace and the remorse needed for Christian unity:

> Everywhere large numbers have felt the impulse of this grace, and among our separated brethren also there increases from day to day a movement, fostered by the grace of the Holy Spirit, for the restoration of unity among all Christians. Taking part in this movement, which is called ecumenical, are those who invoke the Triune God and confess Jesus as Lord and Saviour. They do this not merely as individuals but also as members of the corporate groups in which they have heard the Gospel, and which each regards as his Church and indeed, God's. And yet, almost everyone, though in different ways, longs for the one visible Church of God, a Church truly universal and sent forth to the whole world that the world may be converted to the Gospel and so be saved, to the glory of God.

Introduction

Things have moved rapidly since this was published in 1964. Not only is the Roman Catholic Church having a "dialogue" with the Anglican and Orthodox Churches, but it is having them with the Baptist, Methodist and most of the other Protestant Churches as well. And they, in their turn, are having their own conversations with one another.

It is not possible to discuss the relations between all the churches here. Even so, in tracing the ecumenical efforts of the two churches C.S. Lewis wrote about – the Anglican and the Roman Catholic – we nevertheless touch on problems that are common to all.

Pope Paul VI and Archbishop Michael Ramsey met in Rome in 1966 and pledged their two churches to "sincere efforts to remove the causes of conflict and re-establish unity". To help bring this about they founded the Anglican-Roman Catholic International Commission (ARCIC I) in 1970. This commission of Anglican and Roman Catholic theologians met for thirteen sessions between 1970 and 1981, and their Agreed Statements on "Eucharist", "Ministry and Ordination", and "Authority in the Church" are published under the title *The Final Report* (1982). The section on "Authority" covers a number of things, one of which is the primacy of the Pope – a problem for nearly all non-Roman Catholics.

During his visit to England in 1982, Pope John Paul II met Archbishop Robert Runcie in Canterbury on 29th May and they set up a new commission (ARCIC II) to "study all that hinders the mutual recognition of the ministries of our communions, and to recommend what practical steps will be necessary when, on the basis of our unity of faith, we are able to proceed to the restoration of full communion". Because the doctrine of Justification had been a particular cause of contention at the time of the Reformation, the Commission addressed itself to that question, and their report on this was published as *Salvation and the Church* (1987). This, too, is as relevant to Protestants as it is to those who signed it.

It should be pointed out that, while the Anglican-Roman Catholic International Commission is established by the Pope and the Archbishop of Canterbury, it has no official teaching authority. Its findings will not constitute an agreement between the two churches until each has ratified them. Even so, it is an important and necessary step towards reunion.

The most recent declaration to come from the Anglican and the Roman Catholic Churches has been *One in Hope* (1989). This was signed

Introduction

by Pope John Paul II and Archbishop Robert Runcie during their meeting in Rome during 29th September – 2nd October 1989. In this statement they say: "The question and practice of the admission of women to the ministerial priesthood in some provinces of the Anglican Communion prevents reconciliation between us, even where there is otherwise progress towards agreement in faith on the meaning of the Eucharist and the ordained ministry."

The Roman Catholic Church has always asserted positively its belief in the male priesthood (as has the Orthodox Church), and many Anglicans believe the same. However, the twenty-seven provinces of the Anglican Church are independent, and there is not complete unity of belief about the ordination of women to the priesthood. Although not quite the same issue, some Protestant churches have ordained women to their ministries and this has affected their relations with one another.

Is there, then, any reason to hope? To some all these joint declarations and the like will seem little more than a catalogue of failures, a death warrant against any possible chance of unity. The truth is that the efforts to acquire unity have not created more problems than we already had, but revealed those that were already there. This is why those who want to rush ahead and behave as though the problems didn't exist will do little for the cause of truth. One of the finest things about Lewis's "Christian Reunion" is its lack of facile optimism and a willingness to diagnose problems before attempting a cure. Besides this, now that we know what the churches differ about we can also see more clearly than before what they *agree* on – that enormous common ground of truth that Lewis called "Mere Christianity".

In introducing the remaining essays in this book, I do not feel that I am turning from unity to a different subject. Quite the contrary, for there are thousands of Christians of different communions who owe much of the "heavenly unity" they have acquired to Lewis's writings. Here, then, are some which they may not have been able to read because they have been out of print for a number of years.

(2) "Lilies that Fester" was originally published in *Twentieth Century*, vol. CLVII (April 1955). The remaining essays appeared at one time in *Undeceptions: Essays on Theology and Ethics* (1971), and they are the only ones from that collection which have not been reprinted in a Fount Paperback until now: (3) "Evil and God" was reprinted from *The Spectator*, vol. CLXVI (7th February 1941); (4)

Introduction

"Dangers of National Repentance" was originally published in the extinct Church of England newspaper, *The Guardian* (15th March 1940); (5) "Two Ways with the Self" is from *The Guardian* (3rd May 1940); (6) "Meditation on the Third Commandment" is from *The Guardian* (10th January 1941); (7) "Scraps" originally appeared in the *St James Magazine* (December 1945) of St James' Church, Birkdale, Southport; (8) "Miserable Offenders" was preached at St Matthew's Church, Northampton, on 7th April 1946, and it was published by that church in a booklet called *Five Sermons by Laymen* (April–May 1946).

(9) "Cross-Examination" is my title for an interview Sherwood E. Wirt of the Billy Graham Association had with Lewis in Magdalene College, Cambridge, on 7th May 1963. The interview was originally published in two parts under different titles. The first part was called "I Was Decided Upon", *Decision*, vol. II (September 1963), and the second "Heaven, Earth and Outer Space", *Decision*, vol. II (October 1963).

(10) "Behind the Scenes" comes from *Time and Tide*, vol. XXXVII (1st December 1956); (11) "What Christmas Means to Me" is reprinted from *Twentieth Century*, vol. CLXII

Christian Reunion

(December 1957); and (12) "Delinquents in the Snow" appeared first in *Time and Tide*, vol. XXXVIII (7th December 1957).

1 January 1990   Walter Hooper

1

CHRISTIAN REUNION

AN ANGLICAN SPEAKS TO
ROMAN CATHOLICS

I have been asked to write on Christian
reunion: but I am afraid that what I have to say
will amount to little more than a rough analysis
of the actual disunity and a suggestion as to
how most of us ought to behave while our
tragic and sinful divisions continue.

I will begin by saying that, whether for good
or ill, the nature of the disunity has changed
with the centuries: it has become more strictly,
or clearly, theological. I have been well placed
for noticing this because I grew up in a very
archaic society – that of Northern Ireland –
amidst conditions which had even then long
since passed away in England. I have thus had
a glimpse of the *old* disunity – the kind that
descended from the sixteenth century. In it the
strictly theological differences were hopelessly
entangled with differences of nationality, class,
politics, and the less essential differences of
ritual. (I do not suggest that all differences of

ritual are unessential.) They were also very embittered. A Protestant mother whose son turned from Atheism to Rome, or a Roman mother whose son turned from Atheism to Protestantism, would both have felt (I think) simple grief.

That state of affairs has passed away. On the question of ritual, indeed, it has almost turned upside down. In southern England the Romans are now *not ritualistic enough* to please the High Anglicans, and Congregationalists may (I am told) be as "high" as either. Whatever the barrier now is, it is no longer a barrier of candles: whatever the fog, it is not a fog of incense.

And on the purely theological level I think I may say that the barrier is no longer that between a doctrine of Faith and a doctrine of Works. I am not myself convinced that any good Roman every did hold the doctrine of Works in that form of which Protestants accused him, or that any good Protestant ever did hold the doctrine of Faith in that form of which Romans accused him. At any rate I feel certain that no man of good will today hopes to see God either by *Pecca fortiter* or by founding an abbey. It would still be difficult (especially in Germany) to get an agreed formula: but I think that difficulty now springs rather from the mysteriousness of the subject itself than from two clearly held and mutually exclusive doctrines.

The difficulty that remains, and which becomes sharper as it becomes narrower, is our disagreement about the seat and nature of doctrinal Authority. The real reason, I take it, why you cannot be in communion with us is not your disagreement with this or that particular Protestant doctrine, so much as the absence of any real "Doctrine", in your sense of the word, at all. It is, you feel, like asking a man to say he agrees not with a speaker but with a debating society. And the real reason why I cannot be in communion with you is not my disagreement with this or that Roman doctrine, but that to accept your Church means, not to accept a given body of doctrine, but to accept in advance any doctrine your Church hereafter produces. It is like being asked to agree not only to what a man has said but to what he's going to say.

To you the real vice of Protestantism is the formless drift which seems unable to retain the Catholic truths, which loses them one by one and ends in a "modernism" which cannot be classified as Christian by any tolerable stretch of the word. To us the terrible thing about Rome is the recklessness (as we hold) with which she has added to the *depositum fidei* – the tropical fertility, the proliferation, of *credenda*. You see in Protestantism the Faith dying out in a desert: we see in Rome the Faith smothered in a jungle.

I know no way of bridging this gulf. Nor do I think it the business of the private layman to offer much advice on bridge-building to his betters. My only function as a Christian writer is to preach "mere Christianity" not *ad clerum* but *ad populum*. Any success that has been given me has, I believe, been due to my strict observance of those limits. By attempting to do otherwise I should only add one more recruit (and a very ill qualified recruit) to the ranks of the controversialists. After that I should be no more use to anyone.

I have, however, a strong premonition as to the way in which reunion will *not* come. It will not come at the edges. "Liberal" Romans and "high" Anglicans will not be the ones who will meet first. For the odd thing is that the nearer you get to the heart of each communion, the less you notice its difference from the other.

It is important at this point that I should not be misunderstood. What I am trying to say might be interpreted to mean that doctrines "don't matter", and that the essence of the spiritual life lay either in the affections or in some "mystical" experience to which the intelligence is simply irrelevant. I do not believe it is so. That the spiritual life transcends both intelligence and morality, we are probably all agreed. But I suppose it transcends them as poetry transcends grammar, and does not merely exclude them as algebra excludes grammar. I should distrust a mysticism to which they ever became simply irrelevant. That is not the way in which the divisions grow less important at the centre. To the very last, when two people differ in doctrine, logic proclaims that though both might be in error, it is impossible for both to be right. And error always to some extent disables.

When therefore we find a certain heavenly unity existing between really devout persons of differing creeds – a mutual understanding and even a power of mutual edification which each may lack towards a lukewarm member of his own denomination – we must ascribe this to the work of Christ who, in the erroneous one, sterilizes his errors and inhibits the evil consequences they would naturally have ("If ye drink any deadly thing it shall not hurt you" [Mark 16:18]) and opens the eyes of the other party to all the truths mingled in his friend's errors, which are, of course, likely to be truths he particularly needs.

2

LILIES THAT FESTER

In the "Cambridge Number" of the *Twentieth Century* (1955) Mr John Allen asked why so many people "go to such lengths to prove to us that really they are not intellectuals at all and certainly not cultured". I believe I know the answer. Two parallels may help to ease it into the reader's mind.

We all know those who shudder at the word *refinement* as a term of social approval. Sometimes they express their dislike of this usage by facetiously spelling it *refanement*, with the implication that it is likely to be commonest in the mouths of those whose speech has a certain varnished vulgarity. And I suppose we can all understand the shudder, whether we approve it or not. He who shudders feels that the quality of mind and behaviour which we call *refined* is nowhere less likely to occur than among those who aim at, and talk much about, *refinement*. Those who have this quality are not obeying any idea of *refinement* when they abstain from swaggering, spitting, snatching, triumphing, calling names, boasting or contradicting. These modes of behaviour do not occur to them as possibles: if they did, that training and sensibility which constitute refinement would reject them as disagreeables, without reference to any ideal of conduct, just as we reject a bad egg without reference to its possible effect on our stomachs. *Refinement*, in fact, is a name given to certain behaviour from without. From within, it does not appear as *refinement*; indeed, it does not appear, does not become an object of consciousness, at all. Where it is most named it is most absent.

I produce my next parallel with many different kinds of reluctance. But I think it too illuminating to be omitted. The word *religion* is extremely rare in the New Testament or the writings of mystics. The reason is simple. Those attitudes and practices to which we give the collective name of *religion* are themselves concerned with religion hardly at all. To be religious is to have one's attention fixed on God and on one's neighbour in relation to God. Therefore, almost by definition, a religious man, or a man when he is being religious, is not thinking about *religion*; he hasn't the time. *Religion* is what we (or he himself at a later moment) call his activity from outside.

Of course those who disdain the words

refinement and *religion* may be doing so from bad motives; they may wish to impress us with the idea that they are well-bred or holy. Such people are regarding chatter about *refinement* or *religion* simply as symptomatic of vulgarity or worldliness, and eschew the symptom to clear themselves from the suspicion of the disease. But there are others who sincerely and (I believe) rightly think that such talk is not merely a symptom of, but a cause active in producing, that disease. The talk is inimical to the thing talked of, likely to spoil it where it exists and to prevent its birth where it is unborn.

Now *culture* seems to belong to the same class of dangerous and embarrassing words. Whatever else it may mean, it certainly covers deep and genuine enjoyment of literature and the other arts. (By using the word *enjoyment* I do not mean to beg the vexed question about the rôle of pleasure in our experience of the arts. I mean *frui*, not *delectari*; as we speak of a man "enjoying" good health or an estate.) Now if I am certain of anything in the world, I am certain that while a man is, in this sense, enjoying *Don Giovanni* or the *Oresteia* he is not caring one farthing about *culture*. Culture? the irrelevance of it! For just as to be fat or clever means to be fatter or cleverer than most,

24

so to be *cultured* must mean to be more so than most, and thus the very word carries the mind at once to comparisons, and groupings, and life in society. And what has all that to do with the horns that blow as the statue enters, or Clytæmnestra crying, "Now you have named me aright"? In *Howard's End* Mr E. M. Forster excellently describes a girl listening to a symphony. She is not thinking about *culture*: nor about "Music"; nor even about "this music". She sees the whole world through the music. *Culture*, like religion, is a name given from outside to activities which are not themselves interested in *culture* at all, and would be ruined the moment they were.

I do not mean that we are never to talk of things from the outside. But when the things are of high value and very easily destroyed, we must talk with great care, and perhaps the less we talk the better. To be constantly engaged with the idea of *culture*, and (above all) of *culture* as something enviable, or meritorious, or something that confers prestige, seems to me to endanger those very "enjoyments" for whose sake we chiefly value it. If we encourage others, or ourselves, to hear, see, or read great art, on the ground that it is a *cultured* thing to do, we call into play precisely those elements in us which must be in abeyance before we can

25

enjoy art at all. We are calling up the desire for self-improvement, the desire for distinction, the desire to revolt (from one group) and to agree (with another), and a dozen busy passions which, whether good or bad in themselves, are, in relation to the arts, simply a blinding and paralysing distraction.

At this point some may protest that by *culture* they do not mean the "enjoyments" themselves, but the whole habit of mind which such experiences, reacting upon one another, and reflected on, build up as a permanent possession. And some will wish to include the sensitive and enriching social life which, they think, will arise among groups of people who share this habit of mind. But this reinterpretation leaves me with the same difficulty. I can well imagine a lifetime of such enjoyments leading a man to such a habit of mind, but on one condition; namely, that he went to the arts for no such purpose. Those who read poetry to improve their minds will never improve their minds by reading poetry. For the true enjoyments must be spontaneous and compulsive and look to no remoter end. The Muses will submit to no marriage of convenience. The desirable habit of mind, if it is to come at all, must come as a by-product, unsought. The idea of making it one's aim suggests that shattering confidence which Goethe made to Eckermann: "In all my youthful amours the object I had in view was my own ennoblement." To this, I presume, most of us would reply that, even if we believe a love-affair can ennoble a young man, we feel sure that a love-affair undertaken for that purpose would fail of its object. Because of course it wouldn't be a love-affair at all.

So much for the individual. But the claims made for the "cultured" group raise an embarrassing question. What, exactly, is the evidence that *culture* produces among those who share it a sensitive and enriching social life? If by "sensitive" we mean "sensitive to real or imagined affronts", a case could be made out. Horace noted long ago that "bards are a touchy lot". The lives and writings of the Renaissance Humanists and the correspondence in the most esteemed literary periodicals of our own century will show that critics and scholars are the same. But *sensitive* in that meaning cannot be combined with *enriching*. Competitive and resentful egoisms can only impoverish social life. The sensitivity that enriches must be of the sort that guards a man from wounding others, not of the sort that makes him ready to feel wounded himself. Between this sensitivity and *culture*, my own experience does not suggest any causal connection. I have often found it among the uncultured. Among the cultured I have sometimes found it and sometimes not.

Let us be honest. I claim to be one of the cultured myself and have no wish to foul my own nest. Even if that claim is disallowed, I have at least lived among them and would not denigrate my friends. But we are speaking here among ourselves – behind closed doors. Frankness is best. The real traitor to our order is not the man who speaks, within that order, of its faults, but the man who flatters our corporate self-complacency. I gladly admit that we number among us men and women whose modesty, courtesy, fair-mindedness, patience in disputation and readiness to see an antagonist's point of view, are wholly admirable. I am fortunate to have known them. But we must also admit that we show as high a percentage as any group whatever of bullies, paranoiacs and poltroons, of backbiters, exhibitionists, mopes, milksops and world-without-end bores. The loutishness that turns every argument into a quarrel is really no rarer among us than among the sub-literate; the restless inferiority complex ("stern to inflict" but not "stubborn to endure") which bleeds at a touch but scratches like a wildcat is almost as common among us as among schoolgirls.

If you doubt this, try an experiment. Take any one of those who vaunt most highly the adjusting, cleansing, liberating and civilizing effects of *culture* and ask him about other poets, other critics, other scholars, not in the mass but one by one and name by name. Nine times out of ten he will deny of each what he claimed for all. He will certainly produce very few cases in which, on his own showing, *culture* has had its boasted results. Sometimes we suspect that he can think of only one. The conclusion most naturally to be drawn from his remarks is that the praise our order can most securely claim is that which Dr Johnson gave to the Irish. "They are an honest people; they never speak well of one another."

It is then (at best) extremely doubtful whether *culture* produces any of those qualities which will enable people to associate with one another graciously, loyally, understandingly, and with permanent delight. When Ovid said that it "softened our manners", he was flattering a barbarian king. But even if *culture* did all these things, we could not embrace it for their sake. This would be to use consciously and self-consciously, as means to extraneous ends, things which must lose all their power of conducing to those ends by the very fact of being so used. For many modern exponents of *culture* seem to me to be "impudent" in the etymological sense; they lack *pudor*, they have no shyness where men ought to be shy. They handle the most precious and fragile things with the roughness of an auctioneer, and talk of our most intensely solitary and fugitive experiences as if they were selling us a Hoover. It is all really very well summed up in Mr Allen's phrase in the *Twentieth Century* "the faith in culture". A "faith in culture" is as bad as a faith in religion; both expressions imply a turning away from those very things which culture and religion are about. "Culture" as a collective name for certain very valuable activities is a permissible word; but *culture* hypostatised, set up on its own, made into a faith, a cause, a banner, a "platform", is unendurable. For none of the activities in question cares a straw for that faith or cause. It is like a return to early Semitic religion where names themselves were regarded as powers.

Now a step further. Mr Allen complained that, not content with creeping out of earshot when we can bear the voices of certain *culture*-mongers no longer, we then wantonly consort, or pretend that we consort, with the lowest of the low brows, and affect to share their pleasures. There are at this point a good many

allusions which go over my head. I don't know
what A F N is, I am not fond of cellars, and
modern whisky suits neither my purse, my
palate, nor my digestion. But I think I know the
sort of thing he has in mind, and I think I can
account for it. As before, I will begin with a
parallel. Suppose you had spent an evening
among very young and very transparent snobs
who were feigning a discriminating enjoyment
of a great port, though anyone who knew could
see very well that, if they had ever drunk port
in their lives before, it came from a grocer's.
And then suppose that on your journey home
you went into a grubby little teashop and there
heard an old body in a feather boa say to
another old body, with a smack of her lips,
"That was a nice cup o' tea dearie, that was. Did
me good." Would you not, at that moment, feel
that this was like fresh mountain air? For here,
at last, would be something real. Here would be
a mind really concerned about that in which it
expressed concern. Here would be pleasure,
here would be undebauched experience,
spontaneous and compulsive, from the
fountain head. A live dog is better than a dead
lion. In the same way, after a certain kind of
sherry party, where there have been cataracts
of *culture* but never one word or one glance
that suggested a real enjoyment of any art, any

person, or any natural object, my heart warms to the schoolboy on the bus who is reading *Fantasy and Science Fiction*, rapt and oblivious of all the world beside. For here also I should feel that I had met something real and live and unfabricated; genuine literary experience, spontaneous and compulsive, disinterested. I should have hopes of that boy. Those who have greatly cared for any book whatever may possibly come to care, some day, for good books. The organs of appreciation exist in them. They are not impotent. And even if this particular boy is never going to like anything severer than science fiction, even so,

The child whose love is here, at least doth reap
One precious gain, that he forgets himself.

I should still prefer the live dog to the dead lion; perhaps, even, the wild dog to the over-tame poodle or Peke.

I should not have spent so many words on answering Mr Allen's question (neither of us matters sufficiently to justify it) unless I thought that the discussion led to something of more consequence. This I will now try to develop. Mr Forster feels anxious because he dreads Theocracy. Now if he expects to see a Theocracy set up in modern England, I myself

32

believe his expectation to be wholly chimerical. But I wish to make it very clear that, if I thought the thing in the least probable, I should feel about it exactly as he does. I fully embrace the maxim (which he borrows from a Christian) that "all power corrupts". I would go further. The loftier the pretensions of the power, the more meddlesome, inhuman and oppressive it will be. Theocracy is the worst of all possible governments. All political power is at best a necessary evil: but it is least evil when its sanctions are most modest and commonplace, when it claims no more than to be useful or convenient and sets itself strictly limited objectives. Anything transcendental or spiritual, or even anything very strongly ethical, in its pretensions is dangerous, and encourages it to meddle with our private lives. Let the shoemaker stick to his last. Thus the Renaissance doctrine of Divine Right is for me a corruption of monarchy; Rousseau's General Will, of democracy; racial mysticisms, of nationality. And Theocracy, I admit and even insist, is the worst corruption of all. But then I don't think we are in any danger of it. What I think we are really in danger of is something that would be only one degree less intolerable, and intolerable in almost the same way. I would call it Charientocracy; not the rule of the saints but the rule of the χαρίεντες, the *venustiores*, the Hotel de Rambouillet, the Wits, the Polite, the "Souls", the "Apostles", the Sensitive, the *Cultured*, the Integrated, or whatever the latest password may be. I will explain how I think it could come about.

The old social classes have broken up. Two results follow. On the one hand, since most men, as Aristotle observed, do not like to be merely equal with all other men, we find all sorts of people building themselves into groups within which they can feel superior to the mass; little unofficial, self-appointed aristocracies. The *Cultured* increasingly form such a group. Notice their tendency to use the social term *vulgar* of those who disagree with them. Notice that Mr Allen spoke of rebels against, or deserters from, this group, as denying not that they are "intellectual" but that they are "intellectuals", not hiding a quality but deprecating inclusion in a class. On the other hand, inevitably, there is coming into existence a new, real, ruling class: what has been called the Managerial Class. The coalescence of these two groups, the unofficial, self-appointed aristocracy of the *Cultured* and the actual Managerial rulers, will bring us to Charientocracy.

But the two groups are already coalescing,

because education is increasingly the means of access to the Managerial Class. And of course education, in some sense, is a very proper means of access; we do not want our rulers to be dunces. But education is coming to have a new significance. It aspires to do, and can do, far more to the pupil than education (except, perhaps, that of the Jesuits) has ever done before.

For one thing, the pupil is now far more defenceless in the hands of his teachers. He comes increasingly from businessmen's flats or workmen's cottages in which there are few books or none. He has hardly ever been alone. The educational machine seizes him very early and organizes his whole life, to the exclusion of all unsuperintended solitude or leisure. The hours of unsponsored, uninspected, perhaps even forbidden, reading, the ramblings, and the "long, long thoughts" in which those of luckier generations first discovered literature and nature and themselves are a thing of the past. If a Traherne or a Wordsworth were born today he would be "cured" before he was twelve. In short, the modern pupil is the ideal patient for those masters who, not content with teaching a subject, would create a character; helpless Plasticine. Or if by chance (for nature will be nature) he should have any powers of resistance, they know how to deal with him. I am coming to that point in a moment.

Secondly, the nature of the teaching has changed. In a sense it had changed for the better: that is, it demands far more of the master and, in recompense, makes his work more interesting. It has become far more intimate and penetrating; more inward. Not content with making sure that the pupil has read and remembered the text, it aspires to teach him appreciation. It seems harsh to quarrel with what at first sounds so reasonable an aim. Yet there is a danger in it. Everyone now laughs at the old test paper with its context questions and the like, and people ask, "What good can that sort of thing do a boy?" But surely to demand that the test paper should do the boy good is like demanding that a thermometer should heat a room. It was the reading of the text which was supposed to do the boy good; you set the paper to find out if he had read it. And just because the paper did not force the boy to produce, or to feign, appreciation, it left him free to develop in private, spontaneously, as an out-of-school activity which would never earn any marks, such appreciation as he could. That was a private affair between himself and Virgil or himself and Shakespeare. Nine times out of ten, probably, nothing happened at all.

But wherever appreciation did occur (and quite certainly it sometimes did) it was genuine; suited to the boy's age and character; no exotic, but the healthy growth of its native soil and weather. But when we substitute exercises in "practical criticism" for the old, dry papers, a new situation arises. The boy will not get good marks (which means, in the long run, that he will not get into the Managerial Class) unless he produces the kind of responses, and the kind of analytic method, which commend themselves to his teacher. This means at best that he is trained to the precocious anticipation of responses, and of a method, inappropriate to his years. At worst it means that he is trained in the (not very difficult) art of simulating the orthodox responses. For nearly all boys are good mimics. Depend upon it, before you have been teaching for a term, everyone in the form knows pretty well "the sort of stuff that goes down with Prickly Pop-eye". In the old days also they knew what "went down", but the only thing that "went down" was correct answers to factual questions, and there were only two ways of producing those: working or cheating.

The thing would not be so bad if the responses which the pupils had to make were even those of the individual master. But we have already passed that stage. Somewhere (I have not yet tracked it down) there must be a kind of *culture*-mongers' central bureau which keeps a sharp look out for deviationists. At least there is certainly someone who sends little leaflets to schoolmasters, printing half a dozen poems on each and telling the master not only which the pupils must be made to prefer, but exactly on what grounds. (The impertinence of it! We know what Mulcaster or Boyer would have done with those leaflets.)

Thus to say that, under the nascent régime, education alone will get you into the ruling class, may not mean simply that the failure to acquire certain knowledge and to reach a certain level of intellectual competence will exclude you. That would be reasonable enough. But it may come to mean, perhaps means already, something more. It means that you cannot get in without becoming, or without making your masters believe that you have become, a very specific kind of person, one who makes the right responses to the right authors. In fact, you can get in only by becoming, in the modern sense of the word, *cultured*. This situation must be distinguished from one that has often occurred before. Nearly all ruling classes, sooner or later, in some degree or other, have taken up *culture* and patronized the arts. But when that happens the *culture* is the result of their position; one of the luxuries or privileges of their order. The situation we are now facing will be almost the opposite. Entry into the ruling class will be the reward of *culture*. Thus we reach Charientocracy.

Not only is the thing likely to happen; it is already planned and avowed. Mr J. W. Saunders has set it all out in an excellent article entitled "Poetry in the Managerial Age" (*Essays in Criticism*, iv, 3, July 1954). He there faces the fact that modern poets are read almost exclusively by one another. He looks about for a remedy. Naturally he does not suggest that the poets should do anything about it. For it is taken as basic by all the *culture* of our age that whenever artists and audience lose touch, the fault must be wholly on the side of the audience. (I have never come across the great work in which this important doctrine is proved.) The remedy which occurs to Mr Saunders is that we should provide our poets with a conscript audience; a privilege last enjoyed, I believe, by Nero. And he tells us how this can be done. We get our "co-ordinators" through education; success in examinations is the road into the ruling class. All that we need do, therefore, is to make not just poetry, but

Christian Reunion

"the intellectual discipline which the critical reading of poetry can foster", the backbone of our educational system. In other words, practical criticism or something of the sort, exercised, no doubt, chiefly on modern poets, is to be the indispensable subject, failure in which excludes you from the Managerial Class. And so our poets get their conscript readers. Every boy or girl who is born is presented with the choice: "Read the poets whom we, the *cultured*, approve, and say the sort of things we say about them, or be a prole." And this (picking up a previous point) shows how Charientocracy can deal with the minority of pupils who have tastes of their own and are not pure Plasticine. They get low marks. You kick them off the educational ladder at a low rung and they disappear into the proletariat.

Another advantage is that, besides providing poets with a conscript audience for the moment, you can make sure that the regnant literary dynasty will reign almost for ever. For the deviationists whom you have kicked off the ladder will of course include all those troublesome types who, in earlier ages, were apt to start new schools and movements. If there had been a sound Charientocracy in their day, the young Chaucer, the young Donne, the young Wordsworth and Coleridge, could have been dealt with. And thus literary history, as we have known it in the past, may come to an end. Literary man, so long a wild animal, will have become a tame one.

Having explained why I think a Charient-ocracy probable, I must conclude by explaining why I think it undesirable.

Culture is a bad qualification for a ruling class because it does not qualify men to rule. The things we really need in our rulers – mercy, financial integrity, practical intelligence, hard work, and the like – are no more likely to be found in cultured persons than in anyone else.

Culture is a bad qualification in the same way as sanctity. Both are hard to diagnose and easy to feign. Of course not every charientocrat will be a cultural hypocrite nor every theocrat a Tartuffe. But both systems encourage hypocrisy and make the disinterested pursuit of the quality they profess to value more difficult.

But hypocrisy is not the only evil they encourage. There are, as in piety, so in *culture*, states which, if less culpable, are no less disastrous. In the one we have the "Goody-goody"; the docile youth who has neither revolted against nor risen above the routine pietisms and respectabilities of his home. His conformity has won the approval of his parents, his influential neighbours, and his own conscience. He does not know that he has missed anything and is content. In the other, we have the adaptable youth to whom poetry has always been something "Set" for "evaluation". Success in this exercise has given him pleasure and let him into the ruling class. He does not know what he has missed, does not know that poetry ever had any other purpose, and is content.

Both types are much to be pitied: but both can sometimes be very nasty. Both may exhibit spiritual pride, but each in its proper form, since the one has succeeded by acquiescence and repression, but the other by repeated victory in competitive performances. To the pride of the one, sly, simpering and demure, we might apply Mr Allen's word "smug" (especially if we let in a little of its older sense). My epithet for the other would, I think, be "swaggering". It tends in my experience to be raw, truculent, eager to give pain, insatiable in its demands for submission, resentful and suspicious of disagreement. Where the goody-goody slinks and sidles and purrs (and sometimes scratches) like a cat, his opposite number in the ranks of the *cultured* gobbles like an enraged turkey. And perhaps both types are less curable than the hypocrite proper. A hypocrite might (conceivably) repent and mend; or he might be unmasked and rendered innocuous. But who could bring to repentance, and who can unmask, those who were attempting no deception? who don't know that they are not the real thing because they don't know that there ever was a real thing?

Lastly I reach the point where my objections to Theocracy and to Charientocracy are almost identical. "Lilies that fester smell far worse than weeds." The higher the pretensions of our rulers are, the more meddlesome and impertinent their rule is likely to be, and the more the thing in whose name they rule will be defiled. The highest things have the most precarious foothold in our nature. By making sanctity or culture a *moyen de parvenir* you help to drive them out of the world. Let our masters leave these two, at least, alone; leave us some region where the spontaneous, the unmarketable, the utterly private, can still exist.

As far as I am concerned, Mr Allen fell short of the mark when he spoke of a "retreat from the faith in culture". I don't want retreat; I want attack or, if you prefer the word, rebellion. I write in the hope of rousing others to rebel. So far as I can see, the question has nothing to do with the difference between Christians and those who (unfortunately, since the word has long borne a useful, and wholly different, meaning) have been called "humanists". I hope that red herring will not be brought in. I would gladly believe that many atheists and agnostics care for the things I care for. It is for them I have written. To them I say: the "faith in culture" is going to strangle all those things unless we can strangle it first. And there is no time to spare.

3

EVIL AND GOD

(1941)

Dr Joad's article on "God and Evil" last week[1] suggests the interesting conclusion that since neither "mechanism" nor "emergent evolution" will hold water, we must choose in the long run between some monotheistic philosophy, like the Christian, and some such dualism as that of the Zoroastrians. I agree with Dr Joad in rejecting mechanism and emergent evolution. Mechanism, like all materialist systems, breaks down at the problem of knowledge. If thought is the undesigned and irrelevant product of cerebral motions, what reason have we to trust it? As for emergent evolution, if anyone insists on using the word *God* to mean "whatever the universe happens to be going to do next", of course we cannot prevent him. But nobody would in fact so use it unless he had a secret belief that what is coming next will be an improvement. Such a

C. E. M. Joad, "Evil and God", *The Spectator*, vol. CLXVI (31st January 1941), pp. 112–13

belief, besides being unwarranted, presents peculiar difficulties to an emergent evolutionist. If things can improve, this means that there must be some absolute standard of good above and outside the cosmic process to which that process can approximate. There is no sense in talking of "becoming better" if better means simply "what we are becoming" – it is like congratulating yourself on reaching your destination and defining destination as "the place you have reached". Mellontolatry, or the worship of the future, is a *fuddled* religion.

We are left then to choose between monotheism and dualism – between a single, good, almighty source of being, and two equal uncreated, antagonistic Powers, one good and the other bad. Dr Joad suggests that the latter view stands to gain from the "new urgency" of the fact of evil. But *what* new urgency? Evil may seem more urgent to us than it did to the Victorian philosophers – favoured members of the happiest class in the happiest country of the world at the world's happiest period. But it is no more urgent for us than for the great majority of monotheists all down the ages. The classic expositions of the doctrine that the world's miseries are compatible with its creation and guidance by a wholly good Being come from Boethius waiting in prison to be beaten to death, and from St Augustine meditating on the sack of Rome. The present state of the world is normal; it was the last century that was the abnormality.

This drives us to ask why so many generations rejected Dualism. Not, assuredly, because they were unfamiliar with suffering; and not because its obvious *prima facie* plausibility escaped them. It is more likely that they saw its two fatal difficulties, the one metaphysical and the other moral.

The metaphysical difficulty is this. The two Powers, the good and the evil, do not explain each other. Neither Ormuzd nor Ahriman can claim to be the Ultimate. More ultimate than either of them is the inexplicable fact of their being there together. Neither of them chose this *tête-à-tête*. Each of them, therefore, is *conditioned* – finds himself willy nilly in a situation; and either that situation itself, or some unknown force which produced that situation, is the real Ultimate. Dualism has not yet reached the ground of being. You cannot accept two conditioned and mutually independent beings as the self-grounded, self-comprehending Absolute. On the level of picture thinking this difficulty is symbolized by our inability to think of Ormuzd and Ahriman without smuggling in the idea of a common *space* in which they can be together, and thus confessing that we are not yet dealing with the source of the universe but only with two members contained in it. Dualism is a truncated metaphysic.

The moral difficulty is that Dualism gives evil a positive, substantive, self-consistent nature, like that of good. If this were true, if Ahriman existed in his own right no less than Ormuzd, what could we mean by calling Ormuzd good except that we happened to prefer *him*? In what sense can the one party be said to be right and the other wrong? If evil has the same kind of reality as good, the same autonomy and completeness, our allegiance to good becomes the arbitrarily chosen loyalty of a partisan. A sound theory of value demands something very different. It demands that good should be original and evil a mere perversion; that good should be the tree and evil the ivy; that good should be able to see all round evil (as when sane men understand lunacy) while evil cannot retaliate in kind; that good should be able to exist on its own while evil requires the good on which it is parasitic in order to continue its parasitic existence.

The consequences of neglecting this are serious. It means believing that bad men like badness as such, in the same way in which good men like goodness. At first this denial of any common nature between us and our enemies seems gratifying. We call them fiends and feel that we need not forgive them. But, in reality, along with the power to forgive, we have lost the power to condemn. If a taste for cruelty and a taste for kindness were equally ultimate and basic, by what common standard could the one reprove the other? In reality, cruelty does not come from desiring evil as such, but from perverted sexuality, inordinate resentment, or lawless ambition and avarice. That is precisely why it can be judged and condemned from the standpoint of innocent sexuality, righteous anger, and ordinate acquisitiveness. The master can correct a boy's sums because they are blunders in arithmetic – in the same arithmetic which he does and does better. If they were not even attempts at arithmetic – if they were not in the arithmetical world at all – they could not be arithmetical mistakes.

Good and evil, then, are not on all fours. Badness is not even bad *in the same way* in which goodness is good. Ormuzd and Ahriman cannot be equals. In the long run, Ormuzd must be original and Ahriman derivative. The first hazy idea of *devil* must, if we begin to think, be analysed into the more precise ideas of "fallen" and "rebel" angel. But only in the long run. Christianity can go much further with the Dualist than Dr Joad's article seems to suggest. There was never any question of tracing *all* evil to man; in fact, the New Testament has a good deal more to say about dark superhuman powers than about the fall of Adam. As far as this world is concerned, a Christian can share most of the Zoroastrian outlook; we all live between the "fell, incensed points" of Michael and Satan. The difference between the Christian and the Dualist is that the Christian thinks one stage further and sees that if Michael is really in the right and Satan really in the wrong this must mean that they stand in two different relations to somebody or something far further back, to the ultimate ground of reality itself. All this, of course, has been watered down in modern times by the theologians who are afraid of "mythology", but those who are prepared to reinstate Ormuzd and Ahriman are presumably not squeamish on that score.

Dualism can be a manly creed. In the Norse form ("The giants will beat the gods in the end, but I am on the side of the gods") it is nobler by many degrees than most philosophies of the moment. But it is only a half-way house. Thinking along these lines you can avoid

Monotheism, and remain a Dualist, only by refusing to follow your thoughts home. To revive Dualism would be a real step backwards and a bad omen (though not the worst possible) for civilization.

4

DANGERS OF NATIONAL REPENTANCE

(1940)

The idea of national repentance seems at first sight to provide such an edifying contrast to that national self-righteousness of which England is so often accused and with which she entered (or is said to have entered) the last war, that a Christian naturally turns to it with hope. Young Christians especially – last-year undergraduates and first-year curates – are turning to it in large numbers. They are ready to believe that England bears part of the guilt for the present war, and ready to admit their own share in the guilt of England. What that share is, I do not find it easy to determine. Most of these young men were children, and none of them had a vote or the experience which would enable them to use a vote wisely, when England made many of those decisions to which the present disorders could plausibly be traced. Are they, perhaps, repenting what they have in no sense done?

If they are, it might be supposed that their error is very harmless: men fail so often to repent their real sins that the occasional repentance of an imaginary sin might appear almost desirable. But what actually happens (I have watched it happening) to the youthful national penitent is a little more complicated than that. England is not a natural agent, but a civil society. When we speak of England's actions we means the actions of the British Government. The young man who is called upon to repent of England's foreign policy is really being called upon to repent the acts of his neighbour; for a Foreign Secretary or a Cabinet Minister is certainly a neighbour. And repentence presupposes condemnation. The first and fatal charm of national repentance is, therefore, the encouragement it gives us to turn from the bitter task of repenting our own sins to the congenial one of bewailing – but, first, of denouncing – the conduct of others. If it were clear to the young penitent that this is what he is doing, no doubt he would remember the law of charity. Unfortunately the very terms in which national repentance is recommended to him conceal its true nature. By a dangerous figure of speech, he calls the Government not "they" but "we". And since, as penitents, we are not encouraged to be charitable to our own

sins, nor to give ourselves the benefit of any
doubt, a Government which is called "we" is
ipso facto placed beyond the sphere of charity
or even of justice. You can say anything you
please about it. You can indulge in the popular
vice of detraction without restraint, and yet feel
all the time that you are practising contrition. A
group of such young penitents will say, "Let us
repent our national sins"; what they mean is,
"Let us attribute to our neighbour (even our
Christian neighbour) in the Cabinet, whenever
we disagree with him, every abominable
motive that Satan can suggest to our fancy."

Such an escape from personal repentance
into that tempting region

> Where passions have the privilege to work
> And never hear the sound of their own names,[1]

would be welcome to the moral cowardice of
anyone. But it is doubly attractive to the young
intellectual. When a man over forty tries to
repent the sins of England and to love her
enemies, he is attempting something costly; for
he was brought up to certain patriotic
sentiments which cannot be mortified without
a struggle. But an educated man who is now in

[1] Wordsworth, *The Prelude*, XI, 230

his twenties usually has no such sentiment to mortify. In art, in literature, in politics, he has been, ever since he can remember, one of an angry and restless minority; he has drunk in almost with his mother's milk a distrust of English statesmen and a contempt for the manners, pleasures and enthusiasms of his less-educated fellow countrymen. All Christians know that they must forgive their enemies. But "my enemy" primarily means the man whom I am really tempted to hate and traduce. If you listen to young Christian intellectuals talking, you will soon find out who their real enemy is. He seems to have two names – Colonel Blimp and "the businessman". I suspect that the latter usually means the speaker's father, but that is speculation. What is certain is that in asking such people to forgive the Germans and Russians and to open their eyes to the sins of England, you are asking them, not to mortify, but to indulge, their ruling passion. I do not mean that what you are asking them is not right and necessary in itself; we must forgive all our enemies or be damned. But it is emphatically not the exhortation which your audience needs. The communal sins which they should be told to repent are those of their own age and class – its contempt for the uneducated, its readiness to suspect evil, its self-righteous provocations of public obloquy, its breaches of the Fifth Commandment.[2] Of these sins I have heard nothing among them. Till I do, I must think their candour towards the national enemy a rather inexpensive virtue. If a man cannot forgive the Colonel Blimp next door whom he has seen, how shall he forgive the Dictators whom he hath not seen?

Is it not, then, the duty of the Church to preach national repentance? I think it is. But the office – like many others – can be profitably discharged only by those who discharge it with reluctance. We know that a man may have to "hate" his mother for the Lord's sake.[3] The sight of a Christian rebuking his mother, though tragic, may be edifying; but only if we are quite sure that he has been a good son and that, in his rebuke, spiritual zeal is triumphing, not without agony, over strong natural affection. The moment there is reason to suspect that he *enjoys* rebuking her – that he believes himself to be rising above the natural level while he is still, in reality, grovelling below it in the

[2] Honour they father and thy mother; that thy days may be long in the land which the Lord they God giveth thee' Exodus 22:12
[3] Luke 14:26: "If any man come to me, and hate not his father, and mother, and wife, and children, and brethren, and sisters, yea, and his own life also, he cannot be my disciple."

unnatural – the spectacle becomes merely disgusting. The hard sayings of our Lord are wholesome to those only who find them hard. There is a terrible chapter in M. Mauriac's *Vie de Jésus*. When the Lord spoke of brother and child against parent, the other disciples were horrified. Not so Judas. He took to it as a duck takes to water: "*Pourquoi cette stupeur?, se demande Judas ... Il aime dans le Christ cette vue simple, ce regard de Dieu sur l'horreur humaine.*"[4] For there are two states of mind which face the Dominical paradoxes without flinching. God guard us from one of them.

[4] François Mauriac, *Vie de Jésus* (Paris, 1936), ch. 9. " 'Why this stupefaction?' asked Judas ... He loved in Christ his simple view of things, his divine glance at human depravity."

5

TWO WAYS WITH
THE SELF

(1940)

Self-renunciation is thought to be, and indeed
is, very near the core of Christian ethics. When
Aristotle writes in praise of a certain kind of
self-love, we may feel, despite the careful
distinctions which he draws between the
legitimate and the illegitimate *Philautia*,[1] that
here we strike something essentially sub-
Christian. It is more difficult, however, to
decide what we think of St François de Sales's
chapter, *De la douceur envers nous-mêmes*,[2]
where we are forbidden to indulge resentment
even against ourselves and advised to reprove
even our own faults *avec des remonstrances
douces et tranquilles*,[3] feeling more com-
passion than passion. In the same spirit, Lady

[1] *Nicomachean Ethics*, Book 9, ch. 8
[2] Part III, ch. 9 "Of Meekness towards Ourselves" in the
Introduction to the Devout Life (Lyons, 1609)
[3] with mild and calm remonstrances

Julian of Norwich would have us "loving and peaceable", not only to our "even-Christians", but to "ourself".[4] Even the New Testament bids me love my neighbour "as myself",[5] which would be a horrible command if the self were simply to be hated. Yet Our Lord also says that a true disciple must "hate his own life".[6]

We must not explain this apparent contradiction by saying that self-love is right up to a certain point and wrong beyond that point. The question is not one of degree. There are two kinds of self-hatred which look rather alike in their earlier stages, but of which one is wrong from the beginning and the other right to the end. When Shelley speaks of self-contempt as the source of cruelty, or when a later poet says that he has no stomach for the man "who loathes his neighbour as himself", they are referring to a very real and very unChristian hatred of the self which may make diabolical a man whom common selfishness would have left (at least, for a while) merely animal. The hard-boiled economist or psychologist of our own day, recognizing the

[4] *Sixteen Revelations of Divine Love*, ch. 44
[5] Matthew 19:19; 22:39; Mark 12:31, 33; Romans 13:9; Galatians 5:14; James 2:8
[6] Luke 14:26; John 12:25

"ideological taint" or Freudian motive in his own make-up, does not necessarily learn Christian humility. He may end in what is called a "low view" of all souls, including his own, which expresses itself in cynicism or cruelty, or both. Even Christians, if they accept in certain forms the doctrine of total depravity, are not always free from the danger. The logical conclusion of the process is the worship of suffering – for others as well as for the self – which we see, if I read it aright, in Mr David Lindsay's *Voyage to Arcturus*, or that extraordinary vacancy which Shakespeare depicts at the end of *Richard III*. Richard in his agony tries to turn to self-love. But he has been "seeing through" all emotions so long that he "sees through" even this. It becomes a mere tautology: "Richard loves Richard; that is, I am I."[7]

Now, the self can be regarded in two ways. On the one hand, it is God's creature, an occasion of love and rejoicing; now, indeed, hateful in condition, but to be pitied and healed. On the other hand, it is that one self of all others which is called *I* and *me*, and which on that ground puts forward an irrational claim to preference. This claim is to be not only hated, but simply killed; "never", as George

[7] *Richard III*, v, iii, 184

MacDonald says, "to be allowed a moment's respite from eternal death". The Christian must wage endless war against the clamour of the *ego* as *ego*: but he loves and approves selves as such, though not their sins. The very self-love which he has to reject is to him a specimen of how he ought to feel to all selves; and he may hope that when he has truly learned (which will hardly be in this life) to love his neighbour as himself, he may then be able to love himself as his neighbour: that is, with charity instead of partiality. The other kind of self-hatred, on the contrary, hates selves as such. It begins by accepting the special value of the particular self called *me*, then, wounded in its pride to find that such a darling object should be so disappointing, it seeks revenge, first upon that self, then on all. Deeply egoistic, but now with an inverted egoism, it uses the revealing argument, "I don't spare myself" – with the implication "then *a fortiori* I need not spare others" – and becomes like the centurion in Tacitus, *immitior quia toleraverat*.[8]

The wrong asceticism torments the self: the right kind kills the selfness; We must die daily: but it is better to love the self than to love nothing, and to pity the self than to pity no one.

[8] "More relentless because he had endured (it himself)." *Annals*, Book I, section 10, line 14

61

6

MEDITATION ON THE THIRD COMMANDMENT

(1941)

From many letters to *The Guardian*, and from much that is printed elsewhere, we learn of the growing desire for a Christian "party", a Christian "front", or a Christian "platform" in politics. Nothing is so earnestly to be wished as a real assault by Christianity on the politics of the world: nothing, at first sight, so fitted to deliver this assault as a Christian Party. But it is odd that certain difficulties in this programme should be already neglected while the printer's ink is hardly dry on M. Maritain's *Scholasticism and Politics*.[1]

The Christian Party must either confine itself to stating what ends are desirable and what means are lawful, or else it must go further and select from among the lawful means those which it deems possible and efficacious and

[1] J. Maritain, *Scholasticism and Politics*, M. J. Adler (London, 1950)

give to these its practical support. If it chooses the first alternative, it will not be a political party. Nearly all parties agree in professing ends which we admit to be desirable – security, a living wage, and the best adjustment between the claims of order and freedom. What distinguishes one party from another is the championship of means. We do not dispute whether the citizens are to be made happy, but whether an egalitarian or a hierarchical State, whether capitalism or socialism, whether despotism or democracy is most likely to make them so.

What, then, will the Christian Party actually do? Philarchus, a devout Christian, is convinced that temporal welfare can flow only from a Christian life, and that a Christian life can be promoted in the community only by an authoritarian State which has swept away the last vestiges of the hated "Liberal" infection. He thinks Fascism not so much an evil as a good thing perverted, regards democracy as a monster whose victory would be a defeat for Christianity, and is tempted to accept even Fascist assistance, hoping that he and his friends will prove the leaven in a lump of British Fascists.

Stativus is equally devout and equally Christian. Deeply conscious of the Fall and therefore convinced that no human creature can be trusted with more than the minimum power over his fellows, and anxious to preserve the claims of God from any infringement by those of Caesar, he still sees in democracy the only hope of Christian freedom. He is tempted to accept aid from champions of the *status quo* whose commercial or imperial motives bear hardly even a veneer of theism.

Finally, we have Spartacus, also a Christian and also sincere, full of the prophetic and Dominical denunciations of riches, and certain that the "historical Jesus", long betrayed by the Apostles, the Fathers, and the churches, demands of us a Left revolution. And he also is tempted to accept help from unbelievers who profess themselves quite openly to be the enemies of God.

The three types represented by these three Christians presumably come together to form a Christian Party. Either a deadlock ensues (and there the history of the Christian Party ends) or else one of the three succeeds in floating a party and driving the other two, with their followers, out of its ranks. The new party – being probably a minority of the Christians who are themselves a minority of the citizens – will be too small to be effective. In practice, it will have to attach itself to the unChristian party nearest to it in beliefs about means – to the Fascists if Philarchus has won, to the Conservatives if Stativus, to the Communists if Spartacus. It remains to ask how the resulting situation will differ from that in which Christians find themselves today.

It is not reasonable to suppose that such a Christian Party will acquire new powers of leavening the infidel organization to which it is attached. Why should it? Whatever it calls itself, it will represent, not Christendom, but a part of Christendom. The principle which divides it from its brethren and unites it to its political allies will not be theological. It will have no authority to speak for Christianity; it will have no more power than the political skill its members give it to control the behaviour of its unbelieving allies. But there will be a real, and most disastrous, novelty. It will be not simply a *part* of Christendom, but *a part claiming to be the whole*. By the mere act of calling itself the Christian Party it implicitly accuses all Christians who do not join it of apostasy and betrayal. It will be exposed, in an aggravated degree, to that temptation which the Devil spares none of us at any time – the temptation of claiming for our favourite opinions that kind and degree of certainty and authority which really belongs only to our Faith. The danger of mistaking our merely natural, though perhaps legitimate, enthusiasms for holy zeal, is always great. Can any more fatal expedient be devised for increasing it than that of dubbing a small band of Fascists, Communists, or Democrats "the Christian Party"? The demon inherent in every party is at all times ready enough to disguise himself as the Holy Ghost; the formation of a Christian Party means handing over to him the most efficient make-up we can find. And when once the disguise has succeeded, his commands will presently be taken to abrogate all moral laws and to justify whatever the unbelieving allies of the "Christian" Party wish to do. If ever Christian men can be brought to think treachery and murder the lawful means of establishing the *régime* they desire, and faked trials, religious persecution and organized hooliganism the lawful means of maintaining it, it will, surely, be by just such a process as this. The history of the late medieval pseudo-Crusaders, of the Covenanters,[2] of the Orangemen,[3] should be

[2] The bodies of Presbyterians in Scotland who in the sixteenth and seventeenth centuries bound themselves by religious and political oaths to maintain the cause of their religion

[3] Members of the Orange Association (founded in 1795) who defended the cause of Protestantism in Ireland

remembered. On those who add "Thus saith the Lord" to their merely human utterances descends the doom of a conscience which seems clearer and clearer the more it is loaded with sin.

All this comes from pretending that God has spoken when He has not spoken. He will not settle the two brothers' inheritance: "Who made Me a judge or a divider over you?"[4] By the natural light He has shown us what means are lawful: to find out which one is efficacious He has given us brains. The rest He has left to us.

M. Maritain has hinted at the only way in which Christianity (as opposed to schismatics blasphemously claiming to represent it) can influence politics. Nonconformity has influenced modern English history not because there was a Nonconformist Party but because there was a Nonconformist conscience which all parties had to take into account. An interdenominational Christian Voters' Society might draw up a list of assurances about ends and means which every member was expected to exact from any political party as the price of his support. Such a society might claim to represent Christendom far more truly than any

[4] Luke 12:14

"Christian Front"; and for that reason I should be prepared, in principle, for membership and obedience to be obligatory on Christians. "So all it comes down to is pestering M.P.s with letters?" Yes: just that. I think such pestering combines the dove and the serpent. I think it means a world where parties have to take care not to alienate Christians, instead of a world where Christians have to be "loyal" to infidel parties. Finally, I think a minority can influence politics only by "pestering" or by becoming a "party" in the new continental sense (that is, a secret society of murderers and blackmailers) which is impossible to Christians. But I had forgotten. There is a third way – by becoming a majority. He who converts his neighbour has performed the most practical Christian-political act of all.

7

SCRAPS

(1945)

1

"Yes", my friend said. "I don't see why there shouldn't be books in Heaven. But you will find that your library in Heaven contains only some of the books you had on earth." "Which?", I asked. "The ones you gave away or lent." "I hope the lent ones won't still have all the borrowers' dirty thumb-marks", said I. "Oh yes they will", said he. "But just as the wounds of the martyrs will have turned into beauties, so you will find that the thumb-marks have turned into beautiful illuminated capitals or exquisite marginal woodcuts."

2

"The angels", he said, "have no senses; their experience is purely intellectual and spiritual. That is why we know something about God which they don't. There are particular aspects of His love and joy which can be communicated to a created being only by sensuous experience. Something of God which the Seraphim can never quite understand flows into us from the blue of the sky, the taste of honey, the delicious embrace of water whether cold or hot, and even from sleep itself.''

3

"You are always dragging me down", said I to my Body. "Dragging *you* down!" replied my Body. "Well I like that! Who taught me to like tobacco and alcohol? You, of course, with your idiotic adolescent idea of being 'grown-up'. My palate loathed both at first: but you would have your way. Who put an end to all those angry and revengeful thoughts last night? Me, of course, by insisting on going to sleep. Who does his best to keep you from talking too much and eating too much by giving you dry throats and headaches and indigestion? Eh?'' "And what about sex?", said I. "Yes, what about it?", retorted the Body. "If you and your wretched imagination would leave me alone I'd give you no trouble. That's Soul all over; you give me orders and then blame me for carrying them out.''

4

"Praying for particular things", said I, "always seems to me like advising God how to run the world. Wouldn't it be wiser to assume that He knows best?" "On the same principle," said he, "I suppose you never ask a man next to you to pass the salt, because God knows best whether you ought to have salt or not. And I suppose you never take an umbrella, because God knows best whether you ought to be wet or dry." "That's quite different", I protested. "I don't see why", said he. "The odd thing is that He should let us influence the course of events at all. But since He lets us do it in one way, I don't see why He shouldn't let us do it in the other."

8

MISERABLE OFFENDERS

AN INTERPRETATION OF
PRAYER BOOK LANGUAGE

(1946)

One of the advantages of having a written and printed service, is that it enables you to see when people's feelings and thoughts have changed. When people begin to find the words of our service difficult to join in, that is of course a sign that we do not feel about those things exactly as our ancestors. Many people have, as their immediate reaction to that situation, the simple remedy – "Well, change the words" – which would be very sensible if you knew that we are right and our ancestors were wrong. It is always at least worth while to find out who it is that is wrong.

The Lenten season is devoted especially to what the theologians call contrition, and so every day in Lent a prayer is said in which we ask God to give us "contrite hearts".[1] Contrite,

[1] The Lenten Collect

72

as you know, is a word translated from Latin, meaning crushed or pulverized. Now modern people complain that there is too much of that note in our Prayer Book. They do not wish their hearts to be pulverized, and they do not feel that they can sincerely say that they are "miserable offenders".[2] I once knew a regular churchgoer who never repeated the words, "the burden of them (i.e. his sins) is intolerable",[3] because he did not feel that they were intolerable. But he was not understanding the words. I think the Prayer Book is very seldom talking primarily about our feelings; that is (I think) the first mistake we're apt to make about these words "we are miserable offenders". I do not think whether we are feeling miserable or not matters. I think it is using the word miserable in the old sense – meaning an object of pity. That a person can be a proper object of pity when he is not feeling miserable, you can easily understand if you imagine yourself looking down from a height on two crowded express trains that are travelling towards one another along the same line at sixty miles an hour. You can see that in forty seconds there will be a head-on collision.

[2] From the General Confession as used at Morning Prayer and Evening Prayer
[3] The General Confession at the Holy Communion

I think it would be very natural to say about the passengers of these trains, that they were objects of pity. This would not mean that they felt miserable themselves; but they would certainly be proper objects of pity. I think that is the sense in which to take the word "miserable". The Prayer Book does not mean that we should feel miserable, but that if we could see things from a sufficient height above we should all realize that we are in fact proper objects of pity.

As to the other one, about the burden of our sins being intolerable, it might be clearer if we said "unbearable", because that still has two meanings: you say "I cannot bear it", when you mean it gives you great pain, but you also say "That bridge will not bear that lorry" – not meaning "That bridge will feel pain", but "If that lorry goes on to it, it will break and not be a bridge any longer, but a mass of rubble." I wonder if that is what the Prayer Book means; that, whether we feel miserable or not, and however we feel, there is on each of us a load which, if nothing is done about it, will in fact break us, will send us from this world to whatever happens afterwards, not as souls but as broken souls.

But are we really to believe that on each of us there lies something which if not taken off us, will in fact break us? It is very difficult. No man has any natural knowledge of his own inner state and I think that at the beginning we probably find it much easier to understand and believe this about other people than about ourselves. I wonder, would I be safe in guessing that every second person has in his life a terrible problem, conditioned by some other person; either someone you work for, or someone who works for you, either someone among your friends or your relations, or actually someone in your own house, who is making, and has for years made, your life very much more difficult than it need be? – someone who has that fatal flaw in his character, on which again and again all your efforts have been wrecked, someone whose fatal laziness or jealousy or intolerable temper, or the fact that he never tells the truth, or the fact that he will always backbite and bear tales, or whatever the fatal flaw may be, which, whether it breaks him or not, will certainly break you.

There are two stages, I think, in one's approach to this problem. One begins by thinking that if only something external happened; if only after the war you could get a better job, if only you could get a new house or if only your mother-in-law or daughter-in-law was no longer living with you; if something like that happened, then things would really be better. But after a certain age you no longer think that, because you know for a fact, that even if all this happened, your husband would still be sulky and self-centred, your wife jealous or extravagant, or your employer a bully, or someone whom you employ and cannot dispense with, a cheat. You know, that if the war ended and you had a better job and a new house, and your mother-in-law or your daughter-in-law no longer lived with you, there would still be that fatal flaw in "so and so's" character.

Perhaps in one's misery, one lets out to an intimate friend a little of what the real trouble is, and your intimate friend says, "Why do you not speak to him or her? Why not have the matter out? They really cannot be as bad as you think." But you say to yourself "Oh! He doesn't know", for of course you have tried again and again to have the matter out, and you know by bitter experience that it will not do the slightest good. You have tried it so often, and you know that any attempt to have it out will only produce either a scene or a total failure of understanding; or, perhaps worst of all, the other person will be kind and equable, and entirely agree with you, and promise to be different. And then in twenty-four hours everything will be exactly the same as it always has been!

Supposing you are not mistaken, misled by your own anger or something of that sort. Supposing you are fairly near the truth, then you are in one sense getting a glimpse of what God must see all the time, because in a certain sense He's up against these people. He is up against their problem as you are. He also has made excellent plans; He has also again and again done His part, by sending into the world prophets and wise men and at last Himself, His own Son. Again and again His plans too have been shipwrecked by that fatal flaw in people's character. And no doubt He sees much more clearly than we do; but even we can see in the case of other people, that unless something is done about their load it will break them. We can see that under the influence of nagging jealousy, or possessive selfishness, their character is day by day ceasing to be human.

Now take a step further. When God looks into your office, or parish, or school, or hospital, or factory, or home, He sees all these people like that, and of course, sees one more, the one whom you do not see. For we may be quite certain that, just as in other people, there is something on which our best endeavours have again and again been shipwrecked, so in us there is something quite equally fatal, on which their endeavours have again and again been shipwrecked. If we are beginners in the Christian life we have nothing to make the fatal flaw clear to ourselves. Does the person with a smelly breath know it smells? Or does the Club bore know he is a bore? Is there a single man or woman who believes himself or herself to be a bore or temperamentally jealous? Yet the world is pretty well sprinkled with bores and jealous people. If we are like that, everyone else will know it before we do. You ask why your friends have not told you about it. But what if they have? They may have tried again and again; but on every occasion, we thought they were being queer, that they were in a bad temper or simply mistaken. They have tried again and again, and have probably now given it up.

What should be done about it? What is the good of my talking about the fatal flaw if one does not know about it? I think the first step is to get down to the flaws which one does know. I am speaking to Christians. Many of you, no doubt, are very far ahead of me in the Christian way. It is not for me to decide whether you should confess your sins to a priest or not (our Prayer Book leaves that free to all and demands it of none)[4] but if you do not, you should at

least make a list on a piece of paper, and make a
serious act of penance about each one of them.
There is something about the mere words, you
know, provided you avoid two dangers, either
of sensational exaggeration – trying to work
things up and make melodramatic sins out of
small matters – or the opposite danger of
slurring things over. It is essential to use the
plain, simple, old-fashioned words that you
would use about anyone else. I mean words
like theft, or fornication, or hatred, instead of
"I did not mean to be dishonest", or "I was
only a boy then", or "I lost my temper". I think
that this steady facing of what one does know
and bringing it before God, without excuses,
and seriously asking for Forgiveness and Grace,
and resolving as far as in one lies to do better, is
the only way in which we can ever begin to
know the fatal thing which is always there, and
preventing us from becoming perfectly just to
our wife or husband, or being a better
employer or employee. If this process is gone
through, I do not doubt that most of us will
come to understand and to share these old
words like "contrite", "miserable" and
"intolerable".

Does that sound very gloomy? Does

4 See the Exhortation in the service of Holy Communion

Christianity encourage morbid introspection? The alternative is much more morbid. Those who do not think about their own sins make up for it by thinking incessantly about the sins of others. It is healthier to think of one's own. It is the reverse of morbid. It is not even, in the long run, very gloomy. A serious attempt to repent and really to know one's own sins is in the long run a lightening and relieving process. Of course, there is bound to be at first dismay and often terror and later great pain, yet that is much less in the long run than the anguish of a mass of unrepented and unexamined sins, lurking in the background of our minds. It is the difference between the pain of the tooth about which you should go to the dentist, and the simple straightforward pain which you know is getting less and less every moment when you have had the tooth out.

9

CROSS-EXAMINATION[1]

(1963)

Mr Wirt: Professor Lewis, if you had a young friend with some interest in writing on Christian subjects, how would you advise him to prepare himself?

Lewis: I would say if a man is going to write on chemistry, he learns chemistry. The same is true of Christianity. But to speak of the craft itself, I would not know how to advise a man how to write. It is a matter of talent and interest. I believe he must be strongly moved if he is to become a writer. Writing is like a "lust", or like "scratching when you itch". Writing comes as a result of a very strong impulse, and when it does come, I, for one, must get it out.

Mr Wirt: Can you suggest an approach that would spark the creation of a body of Christian

---

[1] This interview with C. S. Lewis, was held on 7th May 1963 in Lewis's rooms in Magdalene College, Cambridge. (The interviewer is Mr Sherwood E. Wirt of the Billy Graham Evangelistic Association Ltd.)

literature strong enough to influence our generation?

Lewis: There is no formula in these matters. I have no recipe, no tablets. Writers are trained in so many individual ways that it is not for us to prescribe. Scripture itself is not systematic; the New Testament shows the greatest variety. God has shown us that he can use any instrument. Balaam's ass, you remember, preached a very effective sermon in the midst of his "hee-haws".[2]

Mr Wirt: A light touch has been characteristic of your writings, even when you are dealing with heavy theological themes. Would you say there is a key to the cultivation of such an attitude?

Lewis: I believe this is a matter of temperament. However, I was helped in achieving this attitude by my studies of the literary men of the Middle Ages, and by the writings of G. K. Chesterton. Chesterton, for example, was not afraid to combine serious Christian themes with buffoonery. In the same way, the miracle plays of the Middle Ages would deal with a sacred subject such as the nativity of Christ, yet would combine it with a farce.

Mr Wirt: Should Christian writers, then, in your opinion, attempt to be funny?

[2] Numbers 1–35

Lewis: No. I think that forced jocularities on spiritual subjects are an abomination, and the attempts of some religious writers to be humorous are simply appalling. Some people write heavily, some write lightly. I prefer the light approach because I believe there is a great deal of false reverence about. There is too much solemnity and intensity in dealing with sacred matters; too much speaking in holy tones.

Mr Wirt: But is not solemnity proper and conducive to a sacred atmosphere?

Lewis: Yes and no. There is a difference between a private devotional life and a corporate one. Solemnity is proper in church, but things that are proper in church are not necessarily proper outside, and vice versa. For example, I can say a prayer while washing my teeth, but that does not mean I should wash my teeth in church.

Mr Wirt: What is your opinion of the kind of writing being done within the Christian Church today?

Lewis: A great deal of what is being published by writers in the religious tradition is a scandal and is actually turning people away from the Church. The liberal writers who are continually accommodating and whittling down the truth of the Gospel are responsible. I cannot understand how a man can appear in print claiming to disbelieve everything that he presupposes when he puts on the surplice. I feel it is a form of prostitution.

Mr Wirt: What do you think of the controversial new book, *Honest To God*, by John Robinson, the Bishop of Woolwich?

Lewis: I prefer being honest to being "honest to God".

Mr Wirt: What Christian writers have helped you?

Lewis: The contemporary book that has helped me the most is Chesterton's *The Everlasting Man*. Others are Edwyn Bevan's book, *Symbolism and Belief*, and Rudolf Otto's *The Idea of the Holy*, and the plays of Dorothy Sayers.[3]

Mr Wirt: I believe it was Chesterton who was asked why he became a member of the Church, and he replied, "To get rid of my sins".

Lewis: It is not enough to want to get rid of one's sins. We also need to believe in the One who saves us from our sins. Not only do we need to recognize that we are sinners; we need to believe in a Saviour who takes away sin. Matthew Arnold once wrote, "Nor does the being hungry prove that we have bread". Because we know we are sinners, it does not

[3] Such as *The Man Born to be King* (London, 1943)

follow that we are saved.

Mr Wirt: In your book *Surprised by Joy* you remark that you were brought into the Faith kicking and struggling and resentful, with eyes darting in every direction looking for an escape.[4] You suggest that you were compelled, as it were, to become a Christian. Do you feel that you made a decision at the time of your conversion?

Lewis: I would not put it that way. What I wrote in *Surprised by Joy* was that "before God closed in on me, I was in fact offered what now appears a moment of wholly free choice."[5] But I feel my decision was not so important. I was the object rather than the subject in this affair. I was decided upon. I was glad afterwards at the way it came out, but at the moment what I heard was God saying, "Put down your gun and we'll talk".

Mr Wirt: That sounds to me as if you came to a very definite point of decision.

Lewis: Well, I would say that the most deeply compelled action is also the freest action. By that I mean, no part of you is outside the action. It is a paradox. I expressed it in *Surprised by Joy* by saying that I chose, yet it really did not

[4] (London, 1955), ch. 14
[5] ibid.

seem possible to do the opposite.[6]

Mr Wirt: You wrote twenty years ago that "A man who was merely a man and said the sort of things Jesus said would not be a great moral teacher. He would either be a lunatic – on a level with the man who says he is a poached egg – or else he would be the Devil of Hell. You must make your choice. Either this man was, and is, the Son of God: or else a madman or something worse. You can shut Him up for a fool, you can spit at Him and kill Him as a demon; or you can fall at His feet and call Him Lord and God. But let us not come with any patronizing nonsense about His being a great human teacher. He has not left that open to us. He did not intend to."[7] Would you say your view of this matter has changed since then?

Lewis: I would say there is no substantial change.

Mr Wirt: Would you say that the aim of Christian writing, including your own writing, is to bring about an encounter of the reader with Jesus Christ?

Lewis: That is not my language, yet it is the purpose I have in view. For example, I have just finished a book on prayer, an imaginary correspondence with someone who raises

[6] ibid.
[7] *Mere Christianity* (London, 1952), Bk II, ch. 3

questions about difficulties in prayer.[8]

Mr Wirt: How can we foster the encounter of people with Jesus Christ?

Lewis: You can't lay down any pattern for God. There are many different ways of bringing people into His Kingdom, even some ways that I specially dislike! I have therefore learned to be cautious in my judgement.

But we can block it in many ways. As Christians we are tempted to make unnecessary concessions to those outside the Faith. We give in too much. Now, I don't mean that we should run the risk of making a nuisance of ourselves by witnessing at improper times, but there comes a time when we must show that we disagree. We must show our Christian colours, if we are to be true to Jesus Christ. We cannot remain silent or concede everything away.

There is a character in one of my children's stories named Aslan, who says, "I never tell anyone any story except his own."[9] I cannot speak for the way God deals with others; I only know how He deals with me personally. Of

---

[8] He is speaking of the book later published as *Letters to Malcolm: Chiefly on Prayer* (London, 1964).

[9] Except for slight variations in the wording, Aslan says this to two children who ask him about other people's lives in *The Horse and His Boy* (London, 1954), ch. 11 and ch. 3

course, we are to pray for spiritual awakening, and in various ways we can do something toward it. But we must remember that neither Paul nor Apollos gives the increase.[10] As Charles Williams once said, "The altar must often be built in one place so that the fire may come down in another place."[11]

Mr Wirt: Professor Lewis, your writings have an unusual quality not often found in discussions of Christian themes. You write as though you enjoyed it.

Lewis: If I didn't enjoy writing I wouldn't continue to do it. Of all my books, there was only one I did not take pleasure in writing.

Mr Wirt: Which one?

Lewis: *The Screwtape Letters*. They were dry and gritty going. At the time, I was thinking of objections to the Christian life, and decided to put them into the form, "That's what the devil would say." But making goods "bad" and bads "good" gets to be fatiguing.

Mr Wirt: How would you suggest a young Christian writer go about developing a style?

[10] I Corinthians 3: 6
[11] This is probably a paraphrase of the line, "Usually the way must be made ready for heaven, and then it will come by some other; the sacrifice must be made ready, and the fire will strike on another altar." Charles Williams, *He Came Down from Heaven* (London, 1938), ch. 2. p. 25.

Lewis: The way for a person to develop a style is (a) to know exactly what he wants to say, and (b) to be sure he is saying exactly that. The reader, we must remember, does not start by knowing what we mean. If our words are ambiguous, our meaning will escape him. I sometimes think that writing is like driving sheep down a road. If there is any gate open to the left or the right the reader will most certainly go into it.

Mr Wirt: Do you believe that the Holy Spirit can speak to the world through Christian writers today?

Lewis: I prefer to make no judgement concerning a writer's direct "illumination" by the Holy Spirit. I have no way of knowing whether what is written is from heaven or not. I do believe that God is the Father of lights – natural lights as well as spiritual lights (James 1: 17). That is, God is not interested only in Christian writers as such. He is concerned with all kinds of writing. In the same way a sacred calling is not limited to ecclesiastical functions. The man who is weeding a field of turnips is also serving God.

Mr Wirt: An American writer, Mr Dewey Beegle, has stated that in his opinion the Isaac Watts hymn, "When I Survey the Wondrous Cross", is more inspired by God than is the

"Song of Solomon" in the Old Testament. What would be your view?

Lewis: The great saints and mystics of the Church have felt just the opposite about it. They have found tremendous spiritual truth in the "Song of Solomon". There is a difference of levels here. The question of the canon is involved. Also we must remember that what is meat for a grown person might be unsuited to the palate of a child.

Mr Wirt: How would you evaluate modern literary trends as exemplified by such writers as Ernest Hemingway, Samuel Beckett and Jean-Paul Sartre?

Lewis: I have read very little in this field. I am not a contemporary scholar. I am not even a scholar of the past, but I am a lover of the past.

Mr Wirt: Do you believe that the use of filth and obscenity is necessary in order to establish a realistic atmosphere in contemporary literature?

Lewis: I do not. I treat this development as a symptom, a sign of a culture that has lost its faith. Moral collapse follows upon spiritual collapse. I look upon the immediate future with great apprehension.

Mr Wirt: Do you feel, then, that modern culture is being de-Christianized?

Lewis: I cannot speak to the political aspects of

the question, but I have some definite views about the de-Christianizing of the Church. I believe that there are many accommodating preachers, and too many practitioners in the Church who are not believers. Jesus Christ did not say, "Go into all the world and tell the world that it is quite right." The Gospel is something completely different. In fact, it is directly opposed to the world.

The case against Christianity that is made out in the world is quite strong. Every war, every shipwreck, every cancer case, every calamity, contributes to making a *prima facie* case against Christianity. It is not easy to be a believer in the face of this surface evidence. It calls for a strong faith in Jesus Christ.

Mr Wirt: Do you approve of men such as Bryan Green and Billy Graham asking people to come to a point of decision regarding the Christian life?

Lewis: I had the pleasure of meeting Billy Graham once. We had dinner together during his visit to Cambridge University in 1955, while he was conducting a mission to students. I thought he was a very modest and a very sensible man, and I liked him very much indeed.

In a civilization like ours, I feel that everyone has to come to terms with the claims of Jesus

Christ upon his life, or else be guilty of inattention or of evading the question. In the Soviet Union it is different. Many people living in Russia today have never had to consider the claims of Christ because they have never heard of those claims.

In the same way, we who live in English-speaking countries have never really been forced to consider the claims, let us say, of Hinduism. But in our Western civilization we are obligated both morally and intellectually to come to grips with Jesus Christ; if we refuse to do so we are guilty of being bad philosophers and bad thinkers.

Mr Wirt: What is your view of the daily discipline of the Christian life – the need for taking time to be alone with God?

Lewis: We have our New Testament regimental orders upon the subject. I would take it for granted that everyone who becomes a Christian would undertake this practice. It is enjoined upon us by Our Lord; and since they are His commands, I believe in following them. It is always just possible that Jesus Christ meant what He said when He told us to seek the secret place and to close the door.[12]

Mr Wirt: What do you think is going to happen

12 Matthew 6: 5–6

in the next few years of history, Mr Lewis?

Lewis: I have no way of knowing. My primary field is the past. I travel with my back to the engine, and that makes it difficult when you try to steer. The world might stop in ten minutes; meanwhile, we are to go on doing our duty. The great thing is to be found at one's post as a child of God, living each day as though it were our last, but planning as though our world might last a hundred years.

We have, of course, the assurance of the New Testament regarding events to come.[13] I find it difficult to keep from laughing when I find people worrying about future destruction of some kind or other. Didn't they know they were going to die anyway? Apparently not. My wife once asked a young woman friend whether she had ever thought of death, and she replied, "By the time I reach that age science will have done something about it!"

Mr Wirt: Do you think there will be widespread travel in space?

Lewis: I look forward with horror to contact with the other inhabited planets, if there are such. We would only transport to them all of our sin and our acquisitiveness, and establish a new colonialism. I can't bear to think of it. But

13 Matthew 24: 4–44; Mark 13: 5–27; Luke 21: 8–33

if we on earth were to get right with God, of course, all would be changed. Once we find ourselves spiritually awakened, we can go to outer space and take the good things with us. That is quite a different matter.

10

BEHIND THE SCENES

(1956)

When I was taken to the theatre as a small boy what interested me most of all was the stage scenery. The interest was not an aesthetic one. No doubt the gardens, balconies and palaces of the Edwardian "sets" looked prettier to me then than they would now, but that had nothing to do with it. Ugly scenery would have served my turn just as well. Still less did I mistake these canvas images for realities. On the contrary, I believed (and wished) all things on the stage to be more artificial than they actually were.

When an actor came on in ordinary modern clothes I never believed he was wearing a real suit with veritable waistcoat and trousers put on in the ordinary way. I thought he was wearing – and I somehow felt he ought to be wearing – some kind of theatrical overalls which were slipped on all in one piece and fastened invisibly up the back. The stage suit ought not to be a suit; it ought to be something quite different which nevertheless (that's where the pleasure comes) looked like a suit from the stalls. Perhaps this is why I continued, even after I was grown up, to believe in the Cold Tea theory; until a real actor pointed out that a man who played a leading part in a London theatre could afford to, and would certainly rather, provide real whisky (if need were) at his own charge than drink a tumbler of cold tea every evening shortly after his dinner.

No. I knew very well that the scenery was painted canvas; that the stage rooms and stage trees, seen from behind, would not look like rooms or trees at all. That was where the interest lay. That was the fascination of our toy theatre at home, where we made our own scenery. You cut out your piece of cardboard in the shape of a tower and you painted it, and then you gummed an ordinary nursery block on to the back to make it stand upright. The rapture was to dart to and fro. You went in front and there was your tower. You went behind and there – raw, brown cardboard and block.

In the real theatre you couldn't go "behind", but you knew it would be the same. The moment the actor vanished into the wings he entered a different world. One knew it was not a world of any particular beauty or wonder;

somebody must have told me – at any rate I
believed – it would be a rather dingy world of
bare floors and whitewashed walls. The charm
lay in the idea of being able thus to pass in and
out of a world by taking three strides.

One wanted to be an actor not (at that age)
for the sake of fame or applause, but simply that
one might have this privilege of transition. To
come from dressing rooms and bare walls and
utilitarian corridors – and to come suddenly –
into Aladdin's cave or the Darlings' nursery or
whatever it was – to become what you weren't
and be where you weren't – this seemed most
enviable.

It was best of all when the door at the back of
the stage room opened to show a little piece of
passage – unreal passage, of course, its panels
only canvas, intended to suggest (which one
knew to be false) that the sham room on the
stage was part of a whole house. "You can see
just a little *peep* of the passage in Looking Glass
House ... and it's very like our passage as far as
you can see, only you know it may be quite
different on beyond." Thus Alice to the Kitten.[1]
But the stage passage did not leave one to
conjecture. One *knew* it was quite different "on
beyond", that it ceased to be a passage at all.

[1] "Lewis Carroll", *Through the Looking-Glass and What
Alice Found There*, ch. 1

I envied the children in stage boxes. If one sat so far to the side as that, then by craning one's neck one might squint along the sham passage and actually see the point at which it ceased to exist: the joint between the real and the apparent.

Years afterwards I was "behind". The stage was set for an Elizabethan play. The back cloth represented a palace front, with a practicable balcony in it. I stood (from one point of view) on that palace balcony; that is (from the other point of view) I stood on a plank supported by trestles looking out through a square hole in a sheet of canvas. It was a most satisfactory moment.

Now what, I wonder, is behind all this? And what, if anything, comes of it? I have no objection to the inclusion of Freudian explanations provided they are not allowed to exclude all others. It may, as I suppose someone will think, be mixed up with infantile curiosities about the female body. It doesn't feel at all like that. "Of course not", they'll reply. "You mustn't expect it to; no more than – let's see what would be a good parallel – why, no more than the stage rooms and forests look (from the front) like a collection of oddly shaped lath-and-canvas objects grouped in front of the dusty, draughty, whitewashed place 'behind'."

The parallel is fairly exact. The complex, worming its way along in the unimaginable Unconscious, and then suddenly transforming itself (and gaining admission only by that transformation) as it steps into the only "mind" I can ever directly know, is really very like the actor, with his own unhistrionic expression, walking along that bare, draughty "off-stage" and then suddenly appearing as Mr Darling in the nursery or Aladdin in the cave.

But oddly enough we could fit the Freudian theory into the pleasure I started with quite as easily as we fit it into the Freudian theory. Is not our pleasure (even I take some) in Depth Psychology itself one instance of this pleasure in the contrast between "behind the scenes" and "onstage"? I begin to wonder whether that theatrical antithesis moves us because it is a ready-made symbol of something universal.

All sorts of things are, in fact, doing just what the actor does when he comes through the wings. Photons or waves (or whatever it is) come towards us from the sun through space. They are, in a scientific sense, "light". But as they enter the air they become "light" in a different sense: what ordinary people call *sunlight* or *day*, the bubble of blue or grey or greenish, luminosity in which we walk about and see. Day is thus a kind of stage set.

Other waves (this time, of air) reach my eardrum and travel up a nerve and tickle my brain. All this is behind the scenes; as soundless as the whitewashed passages are undramatic. Then somehow (I've never seen it explained) they step on to the stage (no one can tell me *where* this stage is) and become, say, a friend's voice or the *Ninth Symphony*. Or, of course, my neighbour's wireless – the actor may come on stage to play a drivelling part in a bad play. But there is always the transformation.

Biological needs, producing, or stimulated by, temporary physiological states, climb into a young man's brain, pass on to the mysterious stage and appear as "Love" – it may be (since all sorts of plays are performed there) the love celebrated by Dante, or it may be the love of a Guido[2] or a Mr Guppy.[3]

We can call this the contrast of Reality and Appearance. But perhaps the fact of having first met it in the theatre will protect us from the threat of derogation which lurks in the word Appearance. For in the theatre of course the play, the "appearance", is the thing. All the backstage "realities" exist only for its sake and

[2] One of the principal characters in Robert Browning's *The Ring and the Book*
[3] A character in Charles Dickens' *Bleak House*

are valuable only in so far as they promote it. A good, neutral parable is Schopenhauer's story of the two Japanese who attend an English theatre. One devoted himself to trying to understand the play although he did not know a word of the language. The other devoted himself to trying to understand how the scenery, lighting and other machinery worked, though he had never been behind the scenes in a theatre. "Here," said Schopenhauer, "you have the philosopher and the scientist."[4] But for "philosopher" he might also have written "poet", "lover", "worshiper", "citizen", "moral agent" or "plain man".

But notice that in two ways Schopenhauer's parable breaks down. The first Japanese could have taken steps to learn English; but have we ever been given any grammar or dictionary, can we find the teacher, of the language in which this universal drama is being performed? Some

[4] Lewis was probably recalling from memory the parable in Arthur Schopenhauer's *Studies in Pessimism* which runs: "Two Chinamen travelling in Europe went to the theatre for the first time. One of them did nothing but study the machinery, and he succeeded in finding out how it was worked. The other tried to get at the meaning of the piece in spite of his ignorance of the language. Here you have the Astronomer and the Philosopher." The parable is found in Schopenhauer's *Essays from the Parerga and Paralipomena*, trans. T. Bailey Saunders (London, 1951), pp. 80–81

(I among them) would say Yes; others would say No; the debate continues. And the second Japanese could have taken steps – could have pulled wires and got introductions – to win admission behind the scenes and see the off-stage things for himself. At the very least he knew there were such things.

We lack both these advantages. Nobody ever can go "behind". No one can, in any ordinary sense, meet or experience a photon, a sound wave or the unconscious. (That may be one reason why "going behind" in the theatre is exciting; we are doing what, in most cases, is impossible.) We are not even, in the last resort, absolutely sure that such things exist. They are constructs, things assumed to account for our experience, but never to be experienced themselves. They may be assumed with great probability; but they are, after all, hypothetical.

Even the off-stage existence of the actors is hypothetical. Perhaps they do not exist before they enter the scene. And, if they do, then, since we cannot go behind, they may, in their off-stage life and character, be very unlike what we suppose and very unlike one another.

11

WHAT CHRISTMAS
MEANS TO ME

(1957)

Three things go by the name of Christmas. One is a
religious festival. This is important and obligatory
for Christians; but as it can be of no interest to
anyone else, I shall naturally say no more about it
here. The second (it has complex historical
connections with the first, but we needn't go into
them) is a popular holiday, an occasion for merry
making and hospitality. If it were my business to
have a "view" on this, I should say that I much
approve of merry making. But what I approve of
much more is everybody minding his own
business. I see no reason why I should volunteer
views as to how other people should spend their
own money in their own leisure among their own
friends. It is highly probable that they want my
advice on such matters as little as I want theirs. But
the third thing called Christmas is unfortunately
everyone's business.

I mean of course the commercial racket. The
interchange of presents was a very small
ingredient in the older English festivity. Mr

Pickwick took a cod with him to Dingley Dell; the reformed Scrooge ordered a turkey for his clerk; lovers sent love gifts; toys and fruit were given to children. But the idea that not only all friends but even all acquaintances should give one another presents, or at least send one another cards, is quite modern and has been forced upon us by the shopkeepers. Neither of these circumstances is in itself a reason for condemning it. I condemn it on the following grounds.

1. It gives on the whole much more pain than pleasure. You have only to stay over Christmas with a family who seriously try to "keep" it (in its third, or commerical aspect) in order to see that the thing is a nightmare. Long before 25th December everyone is worn out – physically worn out by weeks of daily struggle in over-crowded shops, mentally worn out by the effort to remember all the right recipients and to think out suitable gifts for them. They are in no trim for merry making; much less (if they should want to) to take part in a religious act. They look far more as if there had been a long illness in the house.

2. Most of it is involuntary. The modern rule is that anyone can force you to give him a present by sending you a quite unprovoked present of his own. It is almost a blackmail. Who has not heard the wail of despair, and indeed of resentment, when, at the last moment, just as everyone hoped

that the nuisance was over for one more year, the unwanted gift from Mrs Busy (whom we hardly remember) flops unwelcomed through the letter box, and back to the dreadful shops one of us has to go?

3. Things are given as presents which no mortal ever bought for himself – gaudy and useless gadgets, "novelties" because no one was ever fool enough to make their like before. Have we really no better use for materials and for human skill and time than to spend them on all this rubbish?

4. The nuisance. For after all, during the racket we still have all our ordinary and necessary shopping to do, and the racket trebles the labour of it.

We are told that the whole dreary business must go on because it is good for trade. It is in fact merely one annual symptom of that lunatic condition of our country, and indeed of the world, in which everyone lives by persuading everyone else to buy things. I don't know the way out. But can it really be my duty to buy and receive masses of junk every winter just to help the shopkeepers? If the worst comes to the worst I'd sooner give them money for nothing and write it off as a charity. For nothing? Why, better for nothing than for a nuisance.

12

DELINQUENTS IN
THE SNOW

(1957)

Voices "off", outside the front door, annually
remind us (usually at the most inconvenient
moments) that the season of carols has come
again. At my front door they are, once every
year, the voices of the local choir; on the forty-
five other annual occasions they are those of
boys or children who have not even tried to
learn to sing, or to memorize the words of the
piece they are murdering. The instruments they
play with real conviction are the doorbell and
the knocker; and money is what they are after.

I am pretty sure that some of them are the
very same hooligans who trespass in my
garden, rob my orchard, hack down my trees
and scream outside my windows, though
everyone in the neighbourhood knows that
there is serious illness in my family. I am afraid I
deal with them badly in the capacity of "waits".
I neither forgive like a Christian nor turn the
dog on them like an indignant householder. I

pay the blackmail. I give, but give ungraciously, and make the worst of both worlds.

It would be silly to publish this fact (more proper for a confessor's ear) if I did not think that this smouldering resentment, against which I win so many battles but never win the war, was at present very widely shared by law-abiding people. And Heaven knows, many of them have better cause to feel it than I. I have not been driven to suicide like Mr Pilgrim. I am not mourning for a raped and murdered daughter whose murderer will be kept (partly at my expense) in a mental hospital till he gets out and catches some other child. My greatest grievance is trivial in comparison. But, as it raises all the issues, I will tell it.

Not long ago some of my young neighbours broke into a little pavilion or bungalow which stands in my garden and stole several objects – curious weapons and an optical instrument. This time the police discovered who they were. As more than one of them had been convicted of similar crimes before, we had high hopes that some adequately deterrent sentence would be given. But I was warned: "It'll all be no good if the old woman's on the bench." I had, of course, to attend the juvenile court and all fell out pat as the warning had said. The – let us call her – Elderly Lady presided. It was abundantly

107

proved that the crime had been planned and that it was done for gain: some of the swag had already been sold. The Elderly Lady inflicted a small fine. That is, she punished not the culprits but their parents. But what alarmed me more was her concluding speech to the prisoners. She told them that they must, they really must, give up these "stupid pranks".

Of course I must not accuse the Elderly Lady of injustice. Justice has been so variously defined. If it means, as Thrasymachus thought, "the interest of the stronger", she was very just; for she enforced her own will and that of the criminals and they together are incomparably stronger than I.

But if her intention was – and I do not doubt that the road on which such justice is leading us all is paved with good ones – to prevent these boys from growing up into confirmed criminals, I question whether her method was well judged. If they listened to her (we may hope they did not) what they carried away was the conviction that planned robbery for gain would be classified as a "prank" – a childishness which they might be expected to grow out of. A better way of leading them on, without any sense of frontiers crossed, from mere inconsiderate romping and plundering orchards to burglary, arson, rape and murder, would seem hard to imagine.

This little incident seems to me characteristic of our age. Criminal law increasingly protects the criminal and ceases to protect his victim. One might fear that we were moving towards a Dictatorship of the Criminals or (what is perhaps the same thing) mere anarchy. But that is not my fear; my fear is almost the opposite.

According to the classical political theory of this country we surrendered our right of self-protection to the State on condition that the State would protect us. Roughly, you promised not to stab your daughter's murderer on the understanding that the State would catch him and hang him. Of course this was never true as a historical account of the genesis of the State. The power of the group over the individual is by nature unlimited, and the individual submits because he has to. The State, under favourable conditions (they have ceased), by defining that power, limits it and gives the individual a little freedom.

But the classical theory morally grounds our obligation to civil obedience; explains why it is right (as well as unavoidable) to pay taxes, why it is wrong (as well as dangerous) to stab your daughter's murderer. At present the very uncomfortable position is this: the State protects us less because it is unwilling to protect us against criminals at home, and manifestly grows less and less able to protect us against foreign enemies. At the same time it demands from us more and more. We seldom had fewer rights and liberties nor more burdens: and we get less security in return. While our obligations increase their moral ground is taken away.

And the question that torments me is how long flesh and blood will continue to endure it. There was even, not so long ago, a question whether they ought to. No one, I hope, thinks Dr Johnson a barbarian. Yet he maintained that if, under a peculiarity of Scottish law, the murderer of a man's father escapes, the man might reasonably say, "I am amongst barbarians, who ... refuse to do justice ... I am therefore in a state of nature ... I will stab the murderer of my father." (This is recorded in Boswell's *Journal of a Tour to the Hebrides* under 22nd August 1773.)

Much more obviously, on these principles, when the State ceases to protect me from hooligans I might reasonably, if I could, catch and thrash them myself. When the State cannot or will not protect, "nature" is come again and the right of self-protection reverts to the individual. But of course if I could and did I should be prosecuted. The Elderly Lady and her kind who are so merciful to theft would have no mercy on me; and I should be pilloried in the gutter Press as a "sadist" by journalists who neither know nor care what that word or any word, means.

What I fear, however, is not, or not chiefly, sporadic outbreaks of individual vengeance. I am more afraid, our conditions being so like that of the South after the American Civil War, that some sort of Ku-Klux-Klan may appear and that this might eventually develop into something like a Right or Central revolution. For those who suffer are chiefly the provident, the resolute, the men who want to work, who have built up, in the face of implacable discouragement, some sort of life worth preserving and wish to preserve it. That most (by no means all) of them are "middle class" is not very relevant. They do not get their qualities from a class: they belong to that class because they have those qualities. For in a society like ours no stock which has diligence, forethought or talent, and is prepared to practise self-denial, is likely to remain proletarian for more than a generation. They are, in fact, the bearers of what little moral, intellectual or economic vitality remains. They are not nonentities. There is a point at which their patience will snap.

Christian Reunion

The Elderly Lady, if she read this article, would say I was "threatening" – linguistic nicety not being much in her line. If by a *threat* you mean (but then you don't know much English) the conjectural prediction of a highly undesirable event, then I threaten. But if by the word *threat* you imply that I wish for such a result or would willingly contribute to it, then you are wrong. Revolutions seldom cure the evil against which they are directed; they always beget a hundred others. Often they perpetuate the old evil under a new name. We may be sure that, if a Ku-Klux-Klan arose, its ranks would soon be chiefly filled by the same sort of hooligans who provoked it. A Right or Central revolution would be as hypocritical, filthy and ferocious as any other. My fear is lest we should be making it more probable.

This may be judged an article unfit for the season of peace and goodwill. Yet there is a connection. Not all kinds of peace are compatible with all kinds of goodwill, nor do all those who say "Peace, peace" inherit the blessing promised to the peacemakers.[1] The real *pacificus* is he who promotes peace, not he who gasses about it. Peace, peace ... we won't be hard on you ... it was only a boyish prank ...

[1] Matthew 5:9

you had a neurosis ... promise not to do it again ... out of this in the long run I do not think either goodwill or peace will come. Planting new primroses on the primrose path is no long-term benevolence.

There! They're at it again. "Ark, the errol hyngel sings." They're knocking louder. Well, they come but fifty times a year. Boxing Day is only two and a half weeks ahead; then perhaps we shall have a little quiet in which to remember the birth of Christ.